Presented To

_____

By

_____

_____

Dedication

To Mom and Dad,

who always pointed me to God

Rekindled: WARMED BY FIRES OF HOPE

LEAFWOOD
PUBLISHERS

Cover design by Greg Jackson; interior design by Mark Decker

For information contact:
Leafwood Publishers, Abilene, Texas
1-877-816-4455 toll free
www.leafwoodpublishers.com

07 08 09 10 11 12 / 7 6 5 4 3 2 1

Rekindled

WARMED BY FIRES OF HOPE

VIRGIL M. FRY

LEAFWOOD
PUBLISHERS

Abilene, TX

Endorsements

"Fry's collection of poems, quotes and short essays offers helpful reflections and counsel for those experiencing a season of suffering and trials of faith. This book offers comfort and wisdom for understanding and navigating the journey through grief to God."

—**Max Lucado**, New York Times best-selling author

"What a treasure! Once again, Virgil's collection of often simple and powerful quotations and thoughts allows one to know that feelings of grief and pain can be normal; that God is always there to help us cope."

—**Sue Baier**, author of *Bed Number Ten*

"When challenges deplete energy, leaving us in exhaustion or stress...when our soul searches for meaning...when our spirit is consumed with grief and cold shadows...when our hope is clouded by doubt and discouragement, Virgil Fry's *Rekindled* brings a breath of fresh hope, a warm spirit, and a faith to keep on. Whether reading a single quote, a prayer, paragraph or chapter, through his spiritual reflections we are invited into hopeful, courageous, and rekindled living."

—**Tim P. VanDuivendyk**, author of *The Unwanted Gift of Grief: A Ministry Approach*

"You make the flames of fire
your servants"

Psalm 104:4b

Contents

Section Three

Preface

I am by vocation a hospital chaplain. I am by nature one who seeks spiritual meaning in my world. I, like all humans, am in a constant state of formation. I experience those God-given warm fires which offer stability and comfort—family, friends, mentors, relationships—and often those fires blaze out of my control. Then my task is to find faith resources to endure raging fires, and to find deeper life beyond the turmoil. Such fires that alter my arena of comfort are seen as painful, unwelcome intruders. Yet, faith and love trump the harsh times, and God's message of resurrection always rekindles hope.

I'm grateful for this opportunity to share part of my quest with you. It's a quest informed by my high regard for Scripture, my deep roots within the Christian faith community, my appreciation for God's presence in times of silence, and my belief that this life is rich with meaning even in the darkest of times.

There's no way to adequately thank everyone whose fingerprints touch my life and this book. But some people simply must be singled out.

My wife Caryl is my greatest supporter and my greatest teacher. She knows all too well how fires can rage, yet she always finds ways to endure and to turn hard times into blessings for others, especially for me. My adult children Kyle and Kacie also know about raging fires, and how God's guiding hand is ever with them. All three bring me immense joy and purpose in living.

The support of special friends via Lifeline Chaplaincy in Texas, as well as patients, families and staff of the University of Texas M.D. Anderson Cancer Center, is immeasurable. The staff and volunteers of Lifeline are absolutely amazing to me and to the thousands served by their caring hearts and hands.

I'm grateful to Barry Brewer of 21st Century Christian who opened the opportunity for me to publish *Disrupted*. And now to Leonard Allen and Leafwood Publishers for this second body of work, *Rekindled*.

Finally, the honing, editing, and creative process of *Rekindled* is impacted by the gracious assistance of Jason D. Noble, minister, writer, and confidant. More than anyone, he has encouraged me and given impetus to this book's final useful format. Thank you, friend.

Virgil M. Fry

Introduction

This book is a companion to *Disrupted: Finding God in Illness and Loss*, now reprinted by Leafwood. It, like *Disrupted*, contains reflections, poems, and prayers for anyone who knows crisis in the spiritual journey. It has been formatted to be read as single articles that one gravitates toward due to life circumstances, or in its entirety as a theological reflection.

There are three sections, each dealing with an aspect of the element of fire as spiritual metaphor.

> Section one, *Warmed by Fires of Hope*, addresses those fires which are our useful companions in life.

> Section two, *When Fires Rage*, speaks to what happens when fire transitions into a destructive force.

> Section three, *Fires of Hope Rekindled*, returns us to life anew, life altered, life resurrected.

May the God of peace be with you wherever you journey. And may the raging fires always bring you to a place of knowing that God of peace.

Rekindled

SECTION ONE:

Warmed by Fires of Hope

Sharing the Light
Drawing Us Home

Happiness comes in the capacity to feel deeply,
to enjoy simply,
to think freely,
to risk life,
to be needed.

— *Storm Jameson*

Warmed by Fires of Hope

Sharing the Light
Drawing Us Home

Fire. One of the basic elements of earth. Fire has a mysterious allure to humans. Set us around a campfire or near a fireplace, and inevitably our eyes are drawn trance-like to the fire. Its flaming, dancing light taps into a primal connection, and we find ourselves lured into a state of staring.

As a controlled energy, fire is most useful. Its transformational heat is vital to food preparation, even bringing a distinct flavor that we learn to crave. Its light is synonymous with appealing images like coziness, quiet reflection, or shared intimacies. Its warmth is a much sought-after commodity for cold hands and feet on frigid winter days.

Fire is vital to biblical imagery. We encounter its valuable role in stories of sacrifices, soldiers' night time campgrounds, God's presence, or the valued refining of precious metals. In Scripture, fire serves as a light source for cities and individuals, a means of warming oneself—bringing needed comfort and protection. In such passages, fire sustains, protects, and illuminates the people of God.

From your own mind's eye, think of hearths, candlelight dinners, smoked meats, and campfires with friends and family. More than likely, you'll find such images soothing, compelling, and welcome. Even in our electric lit, microwave world, we still are drawn to the fire.

Fire—so capable of bringing utter destruction—is, in its best sense, a welcome friend. It beckons us to come in from the unforgiving cold world, to bask in its warmth and light.

Each of us needs a warm hearth...one that accepts, sustains, comforts, guides, and loves us.

Fire reflects a God who, more than anything, invites us home.

While on the sea hear the terrible roaring;

See how the boat of my life rolls with me;

In fear of death and in deepest of anguish.

Lord, hear my prayer,

watch my soul on the sea.

Ukranian poem

Warmed by Fires of Hope

IN GRATITUDE FOR THE ANCHOR

We have this hope
as an anchor for the soul,
firm and secure.

Hebrews 6:19

I'm occasionally privileged to join my friends Jay and Judee on sailing tours along Los Angeles' Pacific coast. I love the ride, the view, the dolphins, the ocean spray. As my hosts expertly coax the ship into its seafaring role, I am a mere spectator. To experience the joy of sailing, this West Texas flatlander is better off placing his total trust in their experienced hands.

Not many of us are sailors. Most of us are nautically-challenged—totally unfamiliar with the skills to navigate the high seas. If you're like me, you don't know much about boating equipment. Ropes and sails and pulleys and helms...things that appear as outdated as the crank telephone.

There is one piece of sailing equipment known to everyone, however. The anchor. An image that conjures up security. A reminder of being safely moored in spite of raging storms. A tether that insures safety. A metaphor suggesting home, for being taken care of. Plus, it evokes other similar imagery: the solid rock, the firm foundation, the safe harbor, the embracing shelter.

It's pretty obvious. The anchor's role is to hold us in place. In winds or currents or waves, the anchor supplies much-needed stability. Without it: tumult and disorientation. With it: connectedness and centering.

So who serves as your anchor? Who has God quietly placed in your life, keeping you connected and centered, even when life rages and roars?

Perhaps an attentive spouse. Or a parent or child. Or a friend who just seems to know when to call. Or a neighbor who won't let you feel lonely. Or a companion on a similar spiritual quest. Or a particularly caring co-worker. Or a hospital visitor or volunteer. Or even a total stranger, one who is kind and courteous and expects nothing in return.

Isn't it amazing, when we reflect in gratitude, how many treasured anchors we have? And conversely, how many others are on the receiving end of our role as anchor?

The Lord never promised smooth sailing as we engage life. But the promise of an anchor to keep us safely secured until the storm passes—that is promised again and again. As Solzhenitsyn wrote while in prison: "Faith in God may not get you out of the camp, but it is enough to see you through each day."

May you fully feel the presence of God in those sometimes unseen, often under-appreciated, anchors—the ones who give you enough to see you through each day. And may you find joy in being the same for someone else.

Slow down and enjoy life.
It's not only the scenery you miss
by going fast—
you also miss the sense of where you

are going and why.

Eddie Cantor

Warmed by Fires of Hope

A Prayer For Compassion

We love, because He first loved us.

1 John 4:19, NIV

Don't be interested only in your own life,
but be interested in the lives of other people, too.

Phil 2:4 EVD

Lord God,
We confess:
>   our lifestyles are too busy,
>   our focus self-centered,
>   and our world is consumed
>   with fear, greed, and pride.
Sometimes, Lord, we react
>   to the pains of others
>   with a flippant "who cares?"

Yet, in our more receptive times,
>   when Your Voice calls to
>   our innermost beings,
We know with absolute certainty two things
>   we desperately need:

To be loved...and to love.

Hear us, Lord,
    grateful,
        thankful to experience occasional
            breakthrough moments
                of unconditional love.

Be with those whose hearts are broken,
    demoralized by life's blows;
those who mirror to us that unfairness and suffering
    is not lightened by pat answers or avoidance,
    but is made bearable
        because of fellow travelers
           who truly do care,
              and show it.

Walk with us, God.
Our trek is not always easy,
    our vision shortsighted,
        our love often hidden.
May we seek the deeper places
    where our compassions, our joys reflect
You, the God who is Love.
        Amen.

Before God we are all equally wise—
and equally foolish.

Albert Einstein

Warmed by Fires of Hope

CRACKED BELLS, CHIPPED CUPS, AND ME

We have this treasure in clay jars

II Cor. 4:7

It's always fascinated me. The symbol of our nation's freedom is the Liberty Bell, complete with a cracked shell. In elementary school I was told that attempted repairs to the bell never worked. Finally the obvious crack was incorporated into the design. This defect reflects a democracy obtained with flawed humans who made their share of mistakes and miscalculations. And, less-than-perfect humanity remains a visible part of who we Americans are today. Somehow it seems right to "own" that we are like all people—quite useful, beautiful vessels, but vessels whose edges are chipped and cracked.

Now shift your vision to coffee cups. I collect those ceramic, multi-faceted containers for hot beverages (styrofoam is much too practical and plain). The cups come in all sizes and shapes. Some have wording, some represent far away people or places, some have artwork, and some are works of art. But each, regardless of its intrinsic or sentimental value, is susceptible to the curse of being a cup: chipping. The usefulness of a chipped mug doesn't change; yet, even the tiniest chip alters my perception of its beauty and value. Chipped cups are rarely used for serving drinks to guests. Rarely do I select one for my own personal use. I fancy my java served in a symmetrical, visually pleasing cup.

What is it about us? Why do we often only display objects that appear flawless? Why do we choose to present ourselves as those who have their act together—as with-it, unflappable, unbroken people? Is it possible that we appear whole in order to camouflage our unsightly feet of clay?

Writer Henri Nouwen popularized the term "wounded healers." He asserted that faith travelers are strengthened most by fellow travelers who share, rather than hide, their brokenness. God brings a distinct sense of connection and healing into relationships that allow the cracks and chips to be seen, shared, and lightened. Whatever the source of the crack or chip, regardless of the uniqueness of every hurt, there are multitudes of people who can stand beside us—if and when we let them.

Lord, there is much that breaks my heart. Help me when I downplay the cracks and chips in my facade, when I foolishly trust in showing others only the unscathed exterior, when I fail to see that You provide needed encouragement through fellow wounded healers. Thank You for caring for me, even when I feel uniquely abandoned and lonely. In the name of the One who knows brokenness and wholeness, Amen.

Warmed by Fires of Hope

LOSSES ALONG THE WAY: THE ROLE OF GRIEF IN OUR SPIRITUAL JOURNEY

The eternal silence of
these infinite spaces
fills me with dread.

Blaise Pascal

Jesus was moved, often to tears, by the plights of those the world called "losers." And he provided a caring touch, a healing word, and a loving embrace to those who would receive it. He consciously chose to enter the pain of ultimate loss—giving up his body so that resurrection's story could forever change the way the world experiences change.

But it didn't come easily. Easter Sunday's triumphalism cannot be hailed without counting the cost of the previous Thursday, Friday, and Saturday. Gethsemane and Calvary were excruciating, painful moments for Jesus, for his followers, and for his family. Equally debilitating were the subsequent days of seeming defeat when his body lay in a borrowed tomb. "Pain is a tragedy. But it's never only a tragedy. For the Christian, it's always a necessary mile on the long journey to joy" (Larry Crabb in *Shattered Dreams*).

For today, the truth is every worshiper in a church assembly is dealing with loss on some level. And every worshiper needs to hear that the Bible is far from silent on this issue. In fact, it is highly significant to acknowledge that the Christian faith's central symbol is the juxtaposition of a cross and an empty grave.

Of all entities, the church as a corporate body must claim its healing role in letting its members acknowledge the intense pain of losing precious treasures, of feeling disappointment with God not responding to our hopes, dreams, and felt needs. The church must proclaim that the tumult of dealing with loss is not the same as being unfaithful but is, in fact, faithfulness.

Loss and its accompanying grief is a theme of people of faith. Our vocation includes leaving, letting go, joining others going through loss, and calling out to God. We are called as Christians to enter, not avoid, the realm of pain and loss. And we can be certain that the God who knows loss continues to mold us, joining us as a faithful companion on our spiritual journey.

Warmed by Fires of Hope

Always laugh when you can.
It is cheap medicine.

Lord Byron

Warmed by Fires of Hope

You Know It's Time
To End the Hospital Visit When...

You're in the middle of telling a story when a nurse announces, "Visiting time ended three hours ago."

The patient wants you to call the doctor to ask for more IV pain medicine.

You hear yourself saying, "Oh I don't mind staying... I don't have anything else to do anyway."

The patient looks heavenward and whispers, "How long, O Lord, how long?"

You start listing funeral services you have attended.

You ask to see how the surgery site is healing.

The patient asks, "Tell me again who you are?"

The family doesn't laugh at your dozen medical malpractice jokes.

While you're talking the patient calls the nurse to request a "no visitors" sign.

The patient leaves the room for X-rays, and you don't notice.

You remark that anesthesia is for sissies.

You hear a rousing "amen" when you announce you're about to leave.

The patient's fifth yawn is followed by loud snoring.

Warmed by Fires of Hope

I felt it shelter to speak to you.

Emily Dickinson

Warmed by Fires of Hope

QUICK TO LISTEN?

Let everyone be quick to listen,
slow to speak, slow to anger.
Confess your sins to one another,
and pray for one another,
so that you may be healed.

James 1:19; 5:16

You've probably been there. Someone corners you when you least expect it. There's urgency in the voice. Long-hidden pain erupts, and these words come forth: "Can we talk?"

Now comes the hard part. Mental gymnastics begin inside you. Automatically a flight response kicks in. Your mind jumps ahead, trying to steady yourself. You hope your cellphone will ring. You fire off a hidden protest to God: why me? why now?

But wait, this is not one who constantly demands, constantly drains. Empathy surfaces. You hear yourself answering "Sure. Let's sit down over here."

I'm convinced that few events scare us more, or bond us quicker. In such instances we are immediately in touch with our own inadequacies and flaws. We are also in touch with our desire to help a fellow struggler. It is in this arena of shared weaknesses that God appears, asking us both to allow the healing to begin.

In such a scenario, it's easy to want to offer a quick-fix answer. We can certainly shut down the conversation if we respond with:

> You've got to pull yourself up by your bootstraps.
> You're not praying hard enough.
> Why don't you sleep on it and see if you feel better?
> Someday you'll look back on this and laugh.
> Why don't you just quit doing that?
> Always look on the bright side.
> Maybe God is trying to tell you something.

Or, as Franklin Adams muses: Every time we tell anybody to cheer up, things might be worse, we run away for fear we might be asked to specify how.

Our task, rather than running away, is actually:

> To stay put.
> To offer honest, invitational feedback.
> To listen and learn.
> To join in the journey as an encourager.
> To express belief in the capabilities of the struggler.
> To provide the spiritual resources of prayer and Scripture.
> To ask for additional updates later.

Such caregiving is costly and somewhat risky. But caregiving is worth the cost and the risk, for such responses bring God's loving presence into reality, allowing depths of human care to transcend fear and neediness.

And it won't be long until you'll be the one cornering somebody with urgency and pain in your voice, saying "Can we talk?"

Warmed by Fires of Hope

A PRAYER OF BITTERSWEET MOMENTS

And if the oppressed one cries out to me,
I will hear, for I am compassionate.

God in Exodus 22:27

Our Lord God,
How conflicted life can be—
Full of blessings and curses,
Reasons to celebrate, reasons to lament.

In bittersweet moments,
    we resonate with this phrase:
    "A time for everything under the sun."

Walk with us, companion Lord,
As we relish the naming of our blessings,
As we rehearse the unspeakable joys that come
    with each good and pleasant thing.

Walk with us, companion Lord,
As we reluctantly name failures and losses,
As we rehearse the suppressed pains that come
    with each unwelcome and hidden thing.

For it is in remembering and listing
    the pleasant and the unpleasant,
The things we brag about
    and the things we bury,
That we find You
    still being faithful in your love for us.

It surprises us, Lord, that Scripture
    commands us to remember, to re-tell
Stories of redemption and utter defeat,
    of celebration and lament,
      of unity and division,
    of divinity and evil,
      of births and deaths.

Lead us, Immortal One,
    Pillar of Cloud and Fire,
As you led the Israelite children out of bondage.
Open our eyes to your holy, healing hands
    in all of the stories,
Stories that make us who we are,
    and who we are becoming
In your ever-unfolding kingdom of love.

    Amen.

Warmed by Fires of Hope

Life is God's gift to you.
The way you live your life
is your gift to God.

Leo Buscaglia

Warmed by Fires of Hope

A GOD WHO SLEEPS

While they were sailing, Jesus slept

Luke 8:23a

Sleep. It demands a significant percentage of each day. It refuses to be ignored. It can, at times, be reasoned with and occasionally postponed.

Sleep is the driving force behind our productive activities, those that occur during our "waking moments." Scientists who study our sleep habits observe that sleep deprivation clouds thinking and emotional processing. In fact, going long enough without sleep leads to insane behavior.

Eminent psychiatrist Carl Jung extolled the virtue of sleep. He believed it is the vehicle which gives one's unexpressed unconscious a chance to be heard via dreams.

Sleep is historically a euphemism for death. Deceased Israelite leaders are said to be "asleep with their fathers." When Jesus pronounced a young girl's death as sleep, he was laughed at. When he referred to Lazarus as asleep, he had to speak plainly to his disciples: Lazarus is dead.

As a child, I despised going to bed. Taking naps meant wasted playtime. And going to bed at night meant giving in to a state of existence that took away my control. Not to mention the fact that I might miss some activity or conversation that the adults got to enjoy while I was in bed.

But I also know the sweet release of sleep. After a long, tiring day, sleep can be a most welcome guest. And sometimes the rude clang of a morning alarm clock comes much too soon to dismiss this lovable guest. Hospital patients, or those experiencing deep grief, speak of the long nights when sleep doesn't come easily.

So can I visualize God sleeping? I suppose the familiar Psalm 121:8 makes it difficult to think in those terms (He who keeps Israel will neither slumber nor sleep). In Old Testament phraseology, the living Yahweh is presented as the antithesis of a dead, non-existent god.

But Jesus' life story expands the portrait of God's essence. Incarnation reveals a God who not only creates life out of nothing and lives in ethereal spirit realms, but One who also works, sweats, tires, and sleeps. He is able to sleep soundly, even in the middle of a storm. Why? Because He knows not even a storm can alter God's ultimate loving plans.

A God who sleeps? You bet. For such is a God who knows firsthand all my humanity. In fact, He joins me there.

Warmed by Fires of Hope

EBB AND FLOW: COMMUNITY AND SOLITUDE

To be an imitator of God
requires that we come to terms
with the value of quietness,
slowing down,
coming apart from the noise and speed
of today's pace of life.

Charles Swindoll

Introduction: Cuthbert, a 7th century bishop and mystic, is associated with a "tidal island" called Lindisfarne. Twice daily, rising tides separate the island from the mainland. Then, receding tides reconnect the land with the mainland, and activities between the two resume. Cuthbert often spent time on the island alone with God during the times of separation, afterwards returning to model gentleness and hospitality with his community.

Lindisfarne, an island of both doing and being,
chronos and *kairos*—
an island that permits and celebrates
ebb and flow,
connection and isolation,
an island that proclaims both doing and being
as nature's teaching gift to all.

Cuthbert's island resonates within me as a true symbol of foundational, God-inspired living. Its image helps explain the polarities that draw me:

—one to the noise and hustle of community life, invigorated by the energy and activity of movement and building of dreams

—one to the quiet, inner times away from the crowds (or at least limited to one or two like-minded quiet travelers)

Imbalanced times are the most distressing—those times when I get stuck, immobilized, in one of the two extremes. In the first, the noise of daily living is too much, drowning out my ability to hear the still, small Voice. Or, conversely, there are times when it can be too quiet for too long, leaving my anxious thoughts room to spring forth in full array.

So there it is—a spiritual call for balance, on an island that sounds like a great place to call home—for God is there.

And, indeed, my heart is such an island.

When Fires Rage

Creating Chaos
Leaving Despair

I know God will not give me anything I can't handle.
I just wish He didn't trust me so much.

—*Mother Teresa*

When Fires Rage

CREATING CHAOS
LEAVING DESPAIR

*Y*ou've seen it. The charred remains of a fire that has rampaged out of control. It begins on a small scale—a tiny spark, a careless match, an errant lightening bolt, or an evildoer's volatile combination of combustibles.

It ends with forever-changed remains. Nothing touched by such voracious destruction can ever go back and be the same again.

Hospital burn units attend to bodies whose skin has been melted. Fire fighters risk their lives trying to minimize a raging fire's destruction. Forest rangers seek ways to nurture new-growth, replacement trees. Community groups address resettlement needs of displaced fire victims. Houses are rebuilt, clothing and furniture are replaced, family life begins anew.

Life indeed can go on with new beginnings. But the raw truth is this: when fires rage, suffering results. When the fires are at their hottest, when the end of destruction is not clearly seen, we go into crisis mode and seek ways to endure the flames. Finally, when the fires have been brought under control, we grieve over our losses.

Some fires cannot be seen. Some fires are personal: family distress, serious illness, criminal assault, chronic disease, unjust accusations, financial ruin, faith challenges, death of significant persons, loss of independence. Some fires are global: wars, economic downturns, destruction of property, human depravity, malicious deeds, self-serving tyrants or sub-groups, devalued and displaced people.

Such physical assaults impact spiritual realms. Faith is an essential part of surviving, finding hope for better days, and knowing a Power greater than the destroying force we're encountering.

God's people suffer, but they don't suffer alone or without hope. God promises to hear our cries of pain, our anguished pleas, as surely as He hears our words of praise.

How long will you hide
your face from me?" (Psalms 13:1)
—A struggler laments to God

**"I will never leave you
or forsake you"** (Heb 13:5)
—God responds to all seekers

When Fires Rage

EXPECTING THE UNEXPECTED

*H*ere's a couple of profoundly simple thoughts: life is not always fair, and life is unpredictable in spite of our efforts to make it predictable.

We yearn for order; we get chaos. We codify human behavior; we turn rebellious. We try to manage time; we find it passes too quickly. We assume we'll be healthy; we encounter illness. We trust materialism to fulfill us; we discover it's all easily lost.

Not a very upbeat state of this world's existence, is it?

Ken Cope, quoted in Michael Card's *A Sacred Sorrow,* sees it like this:

We live in a fallen world, full of disappointment and loss, and we often feel empty and unfulfilled and incredibly alone. But while God is not there to fix our problems and make the pain go away, he is always walking beside us. In the ongoing journey of life, we are given the opportunity to know God and ourselves through the process of lamenting and grieving.

Lamenting and grieving? Is that allowed in 21st-Century America? Is that biblical? Is it spiritually permissible?

It may be counter-cultural, even in some churches, but lamenting is truly biblical. Bible readers find that faithful followers of Yahweh all encountered seasons of distress. And more than a few of them openly, verbally, took their distresses and disgusts right to the ears of their God.

They knew, they loved, they trusted in a God who was not immobile, not impotent, not distant. They knew God as one knows an actual loving parent, one open to all expressions: praise and dismay, thanksgiving and frustration.

And they are called faithful.

So when life crashes in on us, when dreams shatter into shards, when the doctor delivers startling news, when the house is destroyed by fire, when the stable job is lost, when the friend becomes an enemy, when lack of control depresses our spirits, when the world is overrun with evil: be faithful. Go to the Psalms, particularly the questioning ones, the laments not read in Sunday morning worship services.

Find a trusted, faithful companion. Pray with brutal honesty. Unload the burden, with all its ugly sentiments. There is hope to be found in voiced despair.

Then know, truly know, that our God is one who will always live up to this promise: I will never leave you nor forsake you.

When Fires Rage

A Prayer for Those Experiencing Unfairness

Here bring your wounded hearts,
here tell your anguish;
Earth has no sorrow
that heav'n cannot heal.

From the hymn "Come Ye Disconsolate" by Thomas Moore

Lord,

Please hear my prayer—
A prayer of confession and need, for
I grow weary of life's battles.
I long for safety and protection.
I internalize the unfairness around me.
I envy those whose lives seem perfect.
And I sometimes consider myself
a victim without voice
a pawn of evil forces
a struggler with no resolution in sight.

You know, O Lord, of our turmoils,
of detoured routing
along the roads we travel.

You know of our desire for calm, and predictability,
and control of our own destinies.

We know, O Lord, of our limitations,
of skewed vision that
zooms in on troubles
while overlooking the goodness
that also accompanies our journey.

Like those who have gone before us,
who wrestled with unfair circumstances
who cried out to You
in dark, lonely times
So also we call out
and earnestly ask for the measure of
strength, hope, and love that
can only come from You—
the One who knows us, loves us, sustains us,
and brings us hope and joy
in spite of the unfairness
that permeates our days.

When Fires Rage

A despairing man
should have the devotion
of his friends.

Job 6:14

When Fires Rage

An Appointment to Gripe

As a caring third grade teacher, my wife Caryl continually sought ways to meet her kids' needs. In order to promote one-to-one availability, she made this offer: by written requests students could schedule personal dialogue time with their teacher.

In response to her offer, one of her students turned in a full sheet of paper with these simple words penciled in block letters:

> Mrs. Fry,
> Can I git an appointment to gripe?
>
> Taylor

I never heard the outcome of that session. Knowing my wife, my guess is that Taylor was invited to speak his concerns, issues were re-framed in new perspectives, and Mrs. Fry was seen as an unsung hero. After all, a third grade teacher is the ultimate authority. To have her available one-to-one is pretty impressive stuff.

I shared a photocopy of Taylor's note with a nurse administrator at M.D. Anderson Cancer Center. She immediately posted Taylor's note, misspelling and all, outside her office door. For she knows it's not only third graders who need a safe place to ventilate—it's all of us, even grown-ups functioning in adult roles.

Some of us struggle with this topic. Somewhere down the line, we've heard that griping is equivalent to self-centered whining. That giving voice to our inner feelings is giving in to weakness. That God expects us to endure, quietly and meekly, all of life's blows. That to lift our voice in lament is sinful, or at least a sign of faith deficiency.

From my view, there is a difference between griping and whining. Griping bemoans the circumstances in which we find ourselves, but it recognizes we have a part in our dilemma. Whining dwells on being a helpless victim, one who acknowledges no responsibility, one who feels the world owes him or her fairness and special treatment. With that definition, griping is biblical, whining is not.

The Psalm writers certainly don't hold back, voicing emotions that erupt in the middle of disruptive dilemmas. In fact, some Psalms are so blatantly confrontive that our comfort level is shaken if they're read in a worship service. In corporate worship, we tend to stick to the Psalms of praise and adoration, leaving the "griping" ones for scholars and sufferers to tackle.

But it's important to recognize that the lamenting Psalms come from faith, not doubt. The writers assume a deeply personal relationship with Creator God who, throughout history, has been Savior and brought redemption in multiple ways. It's more than a little significant that Jesus, at the point of his death on a cross, yelled with his last vestige of strength a direct quotation of Psalm 22: "My God, my God, why hast thou forsaken me?"

So often our world gets turned upside down, and we scramble just to cope, much less to function effectively. Perhaps we ought to follow Taylor's lead by asking God in one-to-one prayer, "Can I get an appointment to gripe?"

Thankfully, it will be no problem getting on God's calendar. After all, having the undivided attention of the Ultimate Authority is pretty impressive stuff.

When Fires Rage

You desire to know the art of
living, my friend?
It is contained in one phrase:
make use of suffering.

Henri-Frederic Amiel

When Fires Rage

A Prayer of One Who Thirsts

Like the deer that yearns for running streams,
so my soul is thirsting for you, my God.
My soul is thirsting for God, the living God.
When can I enter to see the face of God?

Psalm 42:1,2

Lord,
My soul thirsts like the parched earth,
earth without water,
earth with no life visible.

How often have I lamented and been anxious about dry land—
hardened ground that yearns
for water to restore its pliability,
to restore is potential for fruitfulness;
a gift denied in the dry season
of cracked earth and unquenched thirst;
a gift returned when the gentle, ample rains come.
It is then that the Spirit says:

"All shall be well, be all that you are,

be fulfilled, be alive."

My soul—my inner being—

in like manner feels the tension of the desert times.
And my soul wonders:
Is the drought from God, from evil, from within myself,
or is it just the time for drought?

Restore, O Lord, with tender and loving hands,
my soul's oneness with You.
For You are the One who sustains me
in times of thirst, before the rains come to renew.
Amen.

Blessed are they who hunger
and thirst for righteousness,
for they shall be filled.

—Matthew 5:6

When Fires Rage

Humor
is also a way
of saying
something
serious.

T.S. Eliot

When Fires Rage

QUESTIONS YOU'D RATHER NOT HEAR FROM THE HOSPITAL BUSINESS OFFICE

...she had spent all she had on physicians

Luke 8:43

- What's the spending limit on your Mastercard?
- Do you know how to apply for a home equity loan?
- Why don't you just go ahead and pay before we file your insurance for you?
- Are you sure you don't have any money in savings?
- Can we have your cell phone number, please?
- Have you asked the doctor if these tests are necessary?
- Do you mind waiting for your credit report before we admit you to the hospital?
- Isn't it funny how much an aspirin costs in the emergency room?
- What do you mean you can't pay all your deductible today?
- Why don't you sit here while I make a few phone calls?
- Do you want the 800 number for Medicare?
- Did you know that you now qualify for food stamps?
- Our collection agency wants to give you a call... what time do you usually eat supper?

When Fires Rage

We must be willing
to get rid of the life we've planned,
so as to have the life
that is waiting for us.

Joseph Campbell

When Fires Rage

THE GOD OF "NOT YET"

Three times I pleaded with the Lord
to take the thorn in my flesh away from me.
But he said to me, "My grace is sufficient for you,
for my power is made perfect in weakness."

II Corinthians 12:8,9

*T*ravel in this life is, at best, precarious.

That sounds deep and philosophical, doesn't it? But it's a reflection of reality that we faith-travelers face daily.

When I journey away from home, plans are made. Schedules are set. Maps are consulted. Phone calls are initiated. Suitcases are packed. Itineraries are finalized. All before my little Kia Sportage leaves the driveway.

And usually, the plans materialize without a glitch.

But occasionally, the trip gets interrupted. Unforeseen, unwelcome events demand rescheduling, rerouting, rethinking. At such times, I have to admit: only a limited amount of control is mine at any moment. There are factors over which I have little or no say.

Such an admission doesn't set well with me, nor probably with you in similar circumstances. Frustration, anger, sorrow, blame, guilt, despair—all are human, natural responses at moments like these. And during the more serious life disruptions, prayers to God are peppered with pleas for help. Help accompanied by some palatable answers to "why this, why now, why me?"

Isn't it amazing that we serve a God who expects us to react this way? Who expects us to love him enough to confront him with our harshest questions? Who firmly but tenderly reminds us that at times the best answer we can receive is "Not yet."

It's not necessarily the answer we want very much, nor is it one with which we agree. But it is the answer that forces us to realize: Stubborn independence gets in the way of all relationships. And none of us can afford the price of total self-sufficiency.

So we continue to travel, sometimes on roads that are well known, sometimes on roads that don't even appear on our maps. And we, like Paul, are made a little more secure with these break-through words, "My grace is sufficient for you."

Lord, Your creation is constantly in the process of redemption. We confess that we are fiercely independent, and that we attempt to skirt growth by trying to over-control everything in our lives. Thank You for caring so deeply about us that You refuse to let us go anywhere alone. For those times of disruption, when we struggle and hurt, give us an extra measure of Your assuring grace...to continue the journey. Through the One who epitomizes love beyond measure, Amen.

When Fires Rage

Courage
is fear
that has said its prayers

Dorothy Bernard

When Fires Rage

A Prayer for Peace

...and the God of peace will be with you

Philippians 4:9b

Lord God,
God of peace,
God of knowledge,
God of grace,
We come before You, diligently seeking from You
that which is severely lacking in our world:
Peace.

On a national level, we are torn with the violence
Of enemies within and foes without,
And often by our own
Self-driven divisiveness.
On an worldwide scale, we are appalled and
distressed by the lack of regard for
human sanctity,
And wonder if Your word of value for all of Your children
will ever be heard by the masses.

We confess, Lord, that the outer battles we humans fight
are the result of our own inner conflicts,
Our own sinful pride, our own drive for power and control,
Our own willful response to hidden fears
And unspoken guilt.

Forgive us, God, when we champion violence as the only
answer to violence.
Forgive us when we demand justice for our enemies
and expect mercy for ourselves.

Help us, Father, to be a people who love You and Your ways,
A people who love much and hate little,
A people who desire and declare Your
healing, reconciliation, and joy,
A people who speak the language of love
And resist the tongue of evil.

We praise and honor You, Lord,
And lay our request at Your feet, and ask for peace within
ourselves, and within our world.
Through the Name of the One who blesses the peacemakers,
Amen.

Where there is sorrow
there is holy ground.

Oscar Wilde

When Fires Rage

THE UNIQUE JOURNEY OF GRIEF: REFLECTIONS

- No one likes to talk about death. Everyone needs to.

- Tears and laughter, sorrow and joy are God's reminders of the richness of love.

- Dealing with grief can bring out the worst—and the best—in families.

- The brutal reality of death is salved by shared stories of earlier days.

- Grieving is a process, one that takes time. And then some more time.

- The more significant the relationship, the deeper the wound, the longer the healing.

- Grief is common to all, but unique to you. There is no "right" way to grieve, only your way.

- Death of a loved one offers an opportunity to consider one's own mortality.

- Eventually, faithfulness to the deceased demands re-engagement with life.

- Getting over grief is impossible... getting through grief isn't.

- Sometimes the best gift offered to one grieving is simply: "I'm willing to talk about anything, anytime."

- Rituals create communities and offer comfort. Avoiding rituals robs us of needed companionship.

- Faith in God doesn't lessen the pain of loss. It does, however, provide direction, meaning, and hope.

- Fellow grievers share a language which outsiders cannot understand.

- Those who try to talk you out of your grief are not evil—just insecure.

- Significant dates will always remain significant and deserve to be honored in some way.

- Those who do not—or cannot—fully grieve are destined to unexpected bouts of anger, depression, and sadness further down the road.

- There is no fast forward button for getting through grief.

- Keeping it together emotionally for the sake of others exacts an exorbitant price on a griever's emotional well being.

- Being in grief is not being crazy. It just feels like it.

When Fires Rage

Give sorrow words:
the grief that does not speak
whispers the o'er fraught heart,
and bids it speak.

Shakespeare

When Fires Rage

A Prayer While It Is Still Dark

Early on the first day of the week, while it was still dark,
Mary Magdalene went to the tomb and saw that the stone
had been removed from the entrance.

John 20:1

Lord,
It's still dark.
We're here, huddled together,
    praying for the clarity of light.

But,
it's still dark.

We sense your Spirit moving.
    We hope for better light.
We believe in Your power to redeem our world.
    We acknowledge our need for reconciliation.

But,
it's still dark.
We experience shafts of light
    breaking through the darkness
    reminding us that goodness still exists
    stirring up our senses with anticipation.

But,
it's still dark.

Like Mary Magdalene, we seek you out
　　while it's still dark.
Like John and Peter, we run to the empty tomb,
　　and hesitate entering,
　　refusing to believe our own eyes.
We tremble at the unknown future
And we see, really see, that our lives
　　will never be the same again.

Be with us, Gentle Lord,
　　while we dwell in the dark,
　　while we rail against it.
We seek the warm rays of compassion
　　and the faith to believe in Your light,

Even though
it's still dark.

Section Three

Fires of Hope Rekindled

Rejoicing again
Renewing our faith

Unless you believe, you will not understand.

Augustine

Fires of Hope Rekindled

REJOICING AGAIN
RENEWING OUR FAITH

*O*nce raging fires die down, we survivors face new obstacles. We are called to get about the business of starting over, sorting through salvageable debris, discarding that which has been taken away, and finding ways to look forward again.

It's not easy to begin anew. Our meaningful structures no longer exist. No clear roadmap shows us the way. Some people spend copious amounts of physic energy trying to re-capture that which fires destroyed, only to find such efforts futile.

Grieving for significant losses is a normal, healthy, biblical response. Those who refuse to let themselves grieve deny themselves spiritual nourishment. And in truth, the grief, the mourning, the need to cry out surfaces in other ways anyway.

Grieving well is learning to let go, learning to say goodbye, learning to trust God's faithfulness.

When fires obliterate, new life begins almost immediately. To our eyes, charred forests appear bleak and lifeless, yet nature refuses to accept obliteration. New plants and new life forms, ever so slowly, rise out of the ruins. Then we see: resurrection is real.

Moving beyond the pain of destructive fires is a slow, plodding process. But in time, with God's creative powers sustaining us, we re-enter life. Life with a newfound appreciation for the past. Life with a rekindled sense of hope for the future.

Such rekindled hope does not come easily, or all at once, or by our self-directed powers of renewal. But real hope does come. The God who resurrects charred forests does no less for charred people.

Once again, the fires of faith and love become our source of new life. A new, refined, richer life than ever before. A life warmed by the fires of hope.

Fires of Hope Rekindled

SOME ALTERNATIVE RESPONSES TO
SUPPORT SOMEONE IN CRISIS

Writing cheerful graffiti on the rocks
in the valley of deep shadows
is no substitution for companionship
with the person who must walk in the shadows.

—Eugene Peterson

Instead of: It's probably not as bad as it seems.
Try: *What helps you get through tough times?*

Instead of: Just pray harder.
Try: *Are there spiritual resources I can help you with?*

Instead of: You shouldn't dwell on the negative.
Try: *It's hard to find anything good at times like this, isn't it?*

Instead of: I don't understand why you're so upset.
Try: *Help me understand what you're going through.*

Instead of: The more you talk about it the worse you'll feel.
Try: *Let me be your sounding board for awhile.*

| Instead of: | Don't you know it could always be worse? |
| Try: | *It probably seems very overwhelming right now to you.* |

| Instead of: | You've got to keep smiling and looking for the positive. |
| Try: | *I'm impressed that you're able to keep going.* |

| Instead of: | Where's your faith? |
| Try: | *Sometimes our faith journey takes mysterious routes, doesn't it?* |

| Instead of: | Everything happens for a good purpose. |
| Try: | *Right now it's probably hard to see any good coming out of this.* |

| Instead of: | Just count your blessings. |
| Try: | *In spite of everything, you seem to have much going for you.* |

| Instead of: | You need to stay busy with other things. |
| Try: | *May I help you talk through your options?* |

| Instead of: | Here's a professional counselor you should call. |
| Try: | *Would you consider seeking additional help?* |

| Instead of: | I know lots of people who've dealt with that. |
| Try: | *Sometimes it helps to find some others who have survived the same thing.* |

| Instead of: | You know we're not supposed to ask why. |
| Try: | *Isn't it amazing how many people of faith also struggled with why?* |

No act of kindness,
no matter how small,
is ever wasted.

Aesop

Fires of Hope Rekindled

GOD IN THE LITTLE THINGS

(written in response to a friend's phone call on a burdensome day)

But God, who comforts the downcast,
comforted us by the arrival of Titus.

II Cor. 7:6

How easy it is, Lord, for me to become
consumed with issues that impact
my little sphere of existence.
How easy to let the instability of today
fuel the fires of worry about tomorrow,
or next week,
or six months from now.

At these moments of crisis obsession, Lord,
You always seem to
bring another into my self-absorbed world,
another who, in gentle and firm ways,
breaks through my shell—
my shell constructed with planks of panic—
and asks:
"How are you, really?"
or "What's the story behind the calm facade?"
or "How may I journey with you, friend?"

or "Do you know how much I cherish our relationship?"

Small things—simple spoken words—get
magnified in untold ways,
Bringing cascading torrents of welcome refreshment—
comfort to my arid, thirsty soul.

Small things that remind me,
again...and yet again,
that Your love transcends crisis,
permeates chaos,
restores broken vessels.

Thank You, Lord, for your Spirit
that guides those who seek You
to follow through with the little things—
the little things born of Your unlimited,
hands-on care and love.
Amen.

We are disturbed not by things,
but by the view we take of them.

Epictetus

Fires of Hope Rekindled

FROM LEMONS TO LEMONADE

I knocked on the hospital room door. Hearing a beckoning voice, I opened the door and entered the room.

There sat Bill, a man in his mid-thirties. Beside him sat his wife we'll call June. They both welcomed me warmly, but only June spoke. My eyes locked onto Bill's swollen face and neck. I quickly surmised that his surgery had but one purpose: to remove his voicebox. Bill could no longer speak nor eat. His life had forever changed.

But the mood of the room was far from sullen. In fact, June and Bill carried on quite a conversation, albeit in non-conventional ways, with me. Bill gestured, wrote notes, made faces, and moved his lips to speak to us. June sometimes interpreted, and was herself an animated communicator. It was obvious that this room housed a couple committed to each other. Now they united in finding new ways to "do life" with vigor.

Bill subsequently wrote about the adjustments he had to make after his life was brutally interrupted by cancer. A real estate agent, he could no longer relate to or interact with people as he once did with his voice. He experienced additional disappointment when told he could no longer eat solid food. Bill's meals now consisted of twice-daily liquid feedings. He responded with deep feelings of grief, resentment at others, and self pity.

Yet, with the encouragement of his wife and family, Bill began to formulate a proactive plan. Rather than sit on the sidelines as a spectator, over time he developed a strategy. Since he could not eat, he focused his mind on which foods sounded best to him. Then he began making recipes in his mind. The first one: perfect chicken soup! After rehabilitation, he implemented his dream. His family and friends were invited to partake of delicious meals whose recipes were concocted in the quiet of a hospital room. Due to numerous requests, he soon compiled a personal recipe book for his grateful diners.

The project became his greatest therapy, his reconnection with people, his spirit's source of revival. He wrote: *Anyone can overcome seemingly insurmountable problems and disappointment if they decide to refuse to be dominated and controlled by outside forces and influences.*

Which Scripture anchored Bill? It was Romans 5:1-5, particularly verses 3 and 4: "*...suffering produces endurance, and endurance produces character, and character produces hope, and hope does not disappoint us.*" At his lowest point, Bill found his faith in God helped him first to grieve his loss, then to reframe his dilemma, and finally to create new ways to engage life.

So what consumes your life today? What drains your energies, worries your mind, gnaws at your soul? Would you, like Bill, consider God's limitless possibilities as signals of hope and good news? And will you, like Bill, with the encouragement from others, consider definitive ways to make lemonade from your life lemons?

Most importantly, will you invite others to enjoy the sparkling lemonade with you?

Fires of Hope Rekindled

May I Ask You Something, Lord?

No man really becomes a fool
until he stops asking questions.

Charles Steinmetz

Do you have any answers for me?

Question to Chaplain Jeff Pugh

Why couldn't it have been me?

Question from a surviving parent

Are you the Messiah, or shall we look for another?

Message from the imprisoned John

Questions pepper our conversations daily. And questions serve many purposes for us.

Sometimes they correct: ....*Aren't you going to finish that?*
Sometimes they coerce: ....*Wouldn't your mother want you to do this?*
Sometimes they manipulate:..*Don't you love me?*
Sometimes they express anger: ....*Why does this have to happen now?*
Sometimes they voice fears:....................................*Does anybody really care?*
Sometimes they deflect confrontation: ....*Is that a new dress?*
Sometimes they seek wisdom: ....*Can you help me understand?*
Sometimes they seek needed honesty: ....*Is this really true?*
Sometimes they question sanity:........................*What else could go wrong?*

Sometimes they seek comfort: .... *Do you believe in me?*
Sometimes they test trust: ....*Can I tell you something?*
Sometimes they invite companionship: .... *May I join you?*
Sometimes they engender learning:.................*Could I explain that to you?*
Sometimes they deepen faith:.............................. *Can you still love me, Lord?*
Sometimes they speak the unspeakable: .... *Where are you, O Lord?*

Questions proclaim truth, probe mysteries, prompt growth. Seekers of spiritual enlightenment are at home with questions. Biblical characters often conversed with questions.

Questions like the psalmist's plaintive "How long, O Lord?" Or Cain's deflective "Am I my brother's keeper?" Or the book of Job's profound query: "Will someone love God for nothing?"

We might at times avoid asking tough questions, thinking it's better to leave well enough alone.

But we cannot—should not—avoid them. For it is in honest questions we find an ever-present, compelling God...a God who not only hears our questions, but answers them with gentleness, tenderness, and wisdom.

Any questions?

There is more faith
in honest doubt,
believe me,
than in half the creeds.

Tennyson

Fires of Hope Rekindled

IF YOU WERE GOD

Have you ever wondered: what would I do in this world if I were God?
How would I act? What would reveal my essence, without taking
away people's capacity to think and to choose for themselves?

If you were God, would you set in motion a creation, one so intricately
woven that ecologically interdependent life forms
continue to sustain and regenerate
and softly reflect on every level
the handiwork of a master designer?

If you were God, would you give people enough space
to fail and succeed, to learn independence and reliance,
without dogging them every step
and without abandoning them altogether
even when they deserved it?

If you were God, would you let your people
have times of unbridled wealth and power
when gold and silver are excessively abundant
and armies without equal
while you the giver gets forgotten?

If you were God, would you occasionally break through
the ordinary and the busy-ness and the mundane
with voices of unlikely messengers

who cry out that justice, mercy and love
are the only true values worth seeking?

If you were God, would you remind people
that the measure of actual power and control
is not in the hands of the authorities or the rich
but instead in the hands of those who love
without strings and serve without pay?

If you were God, would you not only provide
physical sustenance and survival skills,
but also give beyond measure
those things that renew the spirit and
regenerate life when death always seems to win?

If you were God, would you be willing to sacrifice—
in terms that would cause any parent to tremble—
your child to the world
a child who entered as an infant placed in a borrowed trough,
and who ended as an adult placed in a borrowed tomb?

If you were God, would you amaze everyone
with flashes of undeniable light
or with equally undeniable stillness
both of which reflect in undeniable ways
that you love in terms too deep for words?

If you were God, would you?

Fires of Hope Rekindled

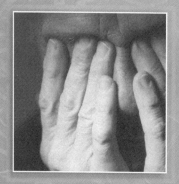

A deep distress

hath humanized my soul.

Wordsworth

Fires of Hope Rekindled

SEEING BEYOND THE OBVIOUS

*T*he early 1960's. My small hometown historically had two schools: one for whites and Hispanics, another for blacks. Department stores had separate restrooms, separate water fountains: one for whites, one for blacks. This primarily agricultural region was only beginning to be affected by the civil rights movement.

When I entered seventh grade, the two schools were merged, or as it was called then, integrated. For the first time, all students walked the same halls, sat in the same classrooms, drank from the same fountains. Uneasiness simmered beneath the surface. In spite of that, faculty and students managed to work together.

Each fall, the community held an annual talent show at the high school auditorium. Students of various levels of talent were provided a forum to entertain an audience of their peers.

Early in the program, the emcee introduced her. The spotlight flashed on, and there she sat: a large African-American high school student behind an imposing electric organ. Most of us did not know her. Snickers rippled across the crowd. She began to sing "Moon River." Laughter erupted. It looked as though she was about to be shamed off the stage.

Undaunted, she continued her song.

Suddenly, the mood of the audience changed. The more this young black woman sang and played, the more awe-struck they became. She ended with a soulful flair. There was no more laughter. There was instead a unified body of students rising to its feet, pleading for an encore. What began as spontaneous rejection became a triumph of acceptance and accolades.

That magic moment changed me. I was never the same after that. I had been willing to dismiss a fellow student's contribution as inferior even before experiencing it. I had been unwilling to see beyond the obvious external facade. I stood convicted.

But it wasn't a turning point for just me. It was a turning point for our school. This young woman's willingness to share herself through music broke down more barriers than the court order which brought about integration. Integration forced us to co-exist reluctantly. She helped us begin to co-exist as community.

There were tears that night. They were mine. Tears that rejoiced that someone had broken through—had taken rejection and turned it around. Tears that recognized in her my own fear of being laughed at, misunderstood, or discounted.

Now I'm a hospital chaplain. Daily I encounter those who, through illness, have change forced upon them. These are my teachers. These who learn not only to endure but to embrace change. These who find in the embrace freedom and transformation. These who risk sharing the music of their liberated spirits with the world.

And I continue to learn: we are all more than we seem. And God continues to call us to see beyond the obvious, to enjoy the music, and to release the fears, and to grow.

Fires of Hope Rekindled

**Trouble makes us one with
every human being in the world.**

Oliver Wendell Holmes

Fires of Hope Rekindled

TROUBLED BY TROUBLES

Do not let your hearts be troubled.
Trust in God; trust also in me.

Jesus, John 14:1

Trouble, troubles, troubled, troubling.
Pivotal, overworked words
    that spring to our lips
    when trying to make sense
       of that
         which seems
           senseless.

We speak of being in trouble
    of having troubles
    of troubled minds
    of troubling news.

We lament that which troubles us,
And seek to regain our equilibrium
    by naming the trouble
    by describing the accompanying feelings
    by looking for solutions.

How appropriate: the essence of faith is

To treat trouble
    as an enemy to be conquered,
    as an ally who teaches, who befriends.

It is difficult, indeed turbulent
To encounter troubles
    while we wish
        for smooth sailing,
        calm waters.

Sailing is seldom smooth,
Waters seldom calm
    as we seek to live, really live,
    and not merely survive
        this trouble-filled voyage
        of life.